The
Edison & Ford
Quote Book

Edison & Ford™
WINTER ESTATES
Homes • Gardens • Laboratory • Museum

ISBN 0-9754824-0-8

Quotations
by
Thomas Alva Edison

Thomas A. Edison.

Thomas Alva Edison Quotations

Genius is 1% inspiration
and 99% perspiration!

As a cure for worrying, work is far
better than whiskey. I always found
that, if I began to worry, the best thing
I could do was focus upon something
useful and then work
very hard at it.

I shall make the electric light so
cheap that only the rich will be
able to burn candles.

A good idea is never lost. Even though its originator or possessor may die, it will someday be reborn in the mind of another. ...Accordingly, my principal business is giving commercial value to the brilliant but misdirected ideas of others.

I have not failed. I've just found 10,000 ways that won't work.

Our greatest weakness lies in giving up. The most certain way to succeed is always to try just one more time.

You will have many opportunities
in life to keep your mouth shut: You
should take advantage of every one
of them.

My philosophy of life is work
– bringing out the secrets of nature
and applying them for the happiness
of man. I know of no better service to
render during the short time we are
in this world.

Everything comes to him who hustles
while he waits.

Restlessness is discontent and
discontent is the first necessity of
progress. Show me a thoroughly
satisfied man I will show you
a failure.

The only time I become discouraged is
when I think of all the things I like to
do and the little time I have in which
to do them.

Good fortune is what happens when
opportunity meets with preparation.

Anything that won't sell, I don't want
to invent. Its sale is proof of utility,
and utility is success.

I never perfected an invention that
I did not think about in terms of the
service it might give others.

To invent, you need a good
imagination and a pile of junk.

All progress, all success springs
from thinking.

I have more respect for the fellow with
a single idea who gets there than for
the fellow with a thousand ideas who
does nothing.

Be courageous. I have seen many
depressions in business. Always
America has emerged from these
stronger and more prosperous.
Be brave as your father before you.
Have faith! Go forward!

Thomas Alva Edison Quotations

The brain can be developed just the same as the muscles can be developed, if one will only take the pains to train the mind to think. Why do so many men never amount to anything? Because they don't think.

Time is really the only capital that any human being has, and the only thing he can't afford to lose.

Because I readily absorb ideas from every source – frequently starting where the last person left off – I am sometimes accurately described as "more of a sponge than an inventor."

Because ideas have to be original
only with regard to their adaptation
to the problem at hand, I am always
interested in novel ideas that others
have used successfully.

Fools call wise men fools. A wise man
never calls any man a fool.

The doctor of the future will give no
medicine, but will interest his patients in
the care of the human body, in diet, and
in the cause and prevention of disease.

Friendship is the leaven of life.

If parents pass enthusiasm along to
their children, they will leave them
an estate of incalculable value.

Being busy does not always mean
real work. The object of all work is
production or accomplishment and
to either of these ends there must
be forethought, system, planning,
intelligence, and honest purpose,
as well as perspiration. Seeming to
do is not doing.

Give me a boy with a willingness to
work and learn and I'll do something
with him. An educated youth that
knows it all is hopeless.

I am proud of the fact that I never
invented weapons to kill.

Results! Why, man, I have gotten a
lot of results. I know several thousand
things that won't work.

Waste is worse than loss. The time is coming when every person who lays claim to ability will keep the question of waste before him constantly. The scope of thrift is limitless.

Non-violence leads to the highest ethics, which is the goal of all evolution. Until we stop harming all other living beings, we are still savages.

Hell, there are no rules here – we're trying to accomplish something.

Opportunity is missed by most people because it comes dressed in overalls and looks like work.

I have friends in overalls whose friendship I would not swap for the favor of the kings of the world.

Great ideas originate in the muscles.

Thomas Alva Edison Quotations

When I have fully decided that a result
is worth getting, I go ahead of it and
make trial after trial until it comes.

Life's most soothing things are a
child's goodnight and sweet music.

Of all my inventions, I like the
phonograph the best.

A man's best friend is a good wife.

I can never pick up a thing
without wishing to improve it.

My philosophy of life: Work and look
on the bright side of everything.

The world owes nothing to any man, but
every man owes something to the world.

I never did anything worth doing
entirely by accident… and almost
none of my inventions came about
totally by accident. They were
achieved by having trained myself
to endure and tolerate hard work.

Many of life's failures are people who
did not realize how close they were to
success when they gave up.

I don't care so much about making my fortune as I do for getting ahead of the other fellows.

One might think that the money value of an invention constitutes its reward to the man who loves his work. But speaking for myself, I can honestly say this is not so. …I continue to find my greatest pleasure, and so my reward, in the work that precedes what the world calls success.

The best thinking has been done in solitude. The worst has been done in turmoil.

Thomas Alva Edison Quotations

I find out what the world needs.
Then I go ahead and try to invent it.

Just because something doesn't
do what you planned it to do
doesn't mean it's useless.

There will one day spring from the
brain of science a machine or force
so fearful in its potentialities, so
absolutely terrifying, that even man,
the fighter, who will dare torture
and death in order to inflict torture
and death, will be appalled, and so
abandon war forever.

From his neck down, a man is worthy
a couple of dollars a day. From his
neck up, he is worth anything that
his brain can produce.

I know this world is ruled by infinite
intelligence. Everything that
surrounds us – everything that exists
– proves that there are infinite laws
behind it. There can be no denying
this fact. It is mathematical in
its precision.

The greatest of all studies
is human nature.

I like my pencil best. A fountain pen
has always been a mystery to me.

Nearly every man who develops an
idea works at it up to the point where
it looks impossible, and then gets
discouraged. That's not the place to
become discouraged.

The value of an idea lies
in the using of it.

I never did a day's work in my life,
it was all fun.

The first requisite for success is the
ability to apply your physical and
mental energies to one problem
incessantly without growing weary.

One generation doesn't profit
by the pain of another.

I never failed once. It just happened to
be a 2000-step process.

My main purpose in life is to make
money so that I can afford to go on
creating more inventions.

If I were a school teacher, I would
put lazy pupils to study bees and ants.
They would soon learn to be diligent.

I owe my success to the fact that I
never had a clock in my workroom.

If we did all the things we are capable
of doing, we would literally astonish
ourselves.

There is far more opportunity
than there is ability.

The three great essentials to achieve
anything worth while are, hard work;
second, stick-to-itiveness; third,
common sense.

It is astonishing what an effort
it seems to be for many people
to put their brains definitely and
systematically to work.

We don't know one millionth of
one percent about anything.

I pity the man without
a purpose in life.

Until man duplicates a blade of grass,
nature can laugh at his so-called
scientific knowledge.

There is no expedient to which
a man will not go to avoid
the labor of thinking.

I am not discouraged because
every wrong attempt discarded
is another step forward.

The chief function of the body
is to carry the brain around.

Your worth consists in what you
are and not in what you have.

I would like to live about three
hundred years. I think I have ideas
enough to keep me busy that long.

There is no substitute for hard work.

What you are will show in what
you do.

Quotations
by
Henry Ford

Henry Ford

Our customers can have a model T in
any color they like, as long as it's black.

Asking "Who ought to be the boss"
is like asking "Who ought to be the
tenor in the quartet?" Obviously, the
man who can sing tenor.

The greatest thing we can produce
is character. Everything else can
be taken away from us.

A business that makes nothing but
money is a poor kind of business.

There is one rule for industrialists and
that is: Make the best quality of goods
possible at the lowest cost possible,
paying the highest wages possible.

Chop your own wood,
and it will warm you twice.

Higher wages are not an additional
cost under proper management.
Better-paid workman are more willing
and more efficient. Better material
is not necessarily more expensive.
On the contrary, it is always more
economical.

A market is never saturated with a
good product, but it is very quickly
saturated with a bad one.

Competition is the great teacher.

All that I personally own of any value is my experience, and that cannot be taken away. One should not complain of having one's fund of experience added to.

The unhappiest man on earth is the one who has nothing to do.

If there is any one secret of success, it lies in the ability to get the other person's point of view and see things from that person's angle as well as from your own.

One of the greatest discoveries a man makes, one of his surprise, is to find he can do what he was afraid he couldn't do.

Anyone who stops learning is old, whether at twenty or eighty. Anyone who keeps learning stays young. The greatest thing in life is to keep your mind young.

Wealth, like happiness, is never attained when sought after directly. It comes as a by-product of providing a useful service.

Beauty appeals to most people.
Beauty begins in design. To me a good
piece of machinery is beautiful. But
when most people speak of beauty they
do not think of quality and fitness of
design, they think of color.

Quality means doing it right
when no one is looking.

One cannot have morale
without cleanliness. We tolerate
makeshift cleanliness no more
than makeshift methods.

Capital punishment is as
fundamentally wrong as a cure for
crime as charity is wrong as a cure
for poverty.

The air is full of ideas. They are
knocking you in the head all the time.
You only have to know what you
want, then forget it, and go about your
business. Suddenly, the idea will come
through. It was there all the time.

Failure is only the opportunity to
begin again more intelligently.

The competitor to be feared is one
who never bothers about you at all,
but goes on making his own business
better all the time.

I know that wars do not end wars.

History is more or less bunk. It's
tradition. We don't want tradition. We
want to live in the present and the only
history that is worth a tinker's damn is
the history we make today.

It is well enough that people
of the nation do not understand
our banking and monetary system,
for if they did, I believe there
would be a revolution before
tomorrow morning.

Life is a series of experiences,
each one of which makes us bigger,
even though sometimes it is hard
to realize this.

Paying attention to simple little things
that most men neglect makes a few
men rich.

Whether you think you can or
think you can't, you're right.

You can take my factories, burn
up my buildings, but give me my
people and I'll build the business
right back again.

Coming together is a beginning.
Keeping together is progress.
Working together is success.

Competition is the keen
cutting edge of business,
always shaving away at costs.

Don't find fault, find a remedy.

Education is not something
to prepare you for life; it is a
continuous part of life.

If you take all the experience and judgment of men over fifty out of our world, there wouldn't be enough left to run it.

Opportunities will not overlook you because you are wearing overalls.

I am looking for a lot of men who have an infinite capacity to not know what can't be done.

I have no patience with professional
charity or with any sort of
commercialized humanitarianism.
The moment human helpfulness is
systematized, organized, commercialized,
and professionalized, the heart of it is
extinguished, and it becomes a cold and
clammy thing.

Time and money spent in helping
men to do more for themselves is far
better than mere giving.

You can do anything if you
have enthusiasm. Enthusiasm is
the yeast that makes your hopes
rise to the stars.

It is all one to me if a man comes form
Sing Sing or Harvard. We hire a man,
not his history.

You say I started out with practically
nothing, but that isn't correct. We all
start with all there is. It's how we use
it that makes things possible.

The highest use of capital is not to
make more money, but to make money
do more for the betterment of life.

There are two fools in this world. One
is the millionaire who thinks that
by hoarding money he can somehow
accumulate real power, and the other
is the penniless reformer who thinks
that if only he can take the money
from one class and give it to another,
all the world's ills will be cured.

If everyone is moving forward together,
then success takes care of itself.

When everything seems to be going
against you, remember that the
airplane takes off against the wind,
not with it.

It has been my observation that most
people get ahead during the time that
others waste.

My best friend is the one who brings
out the best in me.

What I greatly hope for these
children, and for children everywhere,
is a new attitude toward life – free
from the gullibility which thinks
we can get something for nothing;
free from the greed which thinks
any permanent good can come of
overreaching others.

Money doesn't change men, it merely
unmasks them. If a man is naturally
selfish or arrogant or greedy, the
money brings that out, that's all.

An idealist is a person who helps
other people to be prosperous.

Even a mistake may turn out to be the
one thing necessary to a worthwhile
achievement.

If you think of standardization as the
best that you know today, but which is
to be improved tomorrow, you
get somewhere.

Many people think that by hoarding
money they are gaining safety for
themselves. If money is your only hope
for independence, you will never have
it. The only real security that a person
can have in this world is a reserve of
knowledge, experience, and ability.
Without these qualities, money is
practically useless.

Nobody can think straight who does
not work. Idleness warps the mind.

The man who will use his skill and
constructive imagination to see how
much he can give for a dollar, instead
of how little he can give for a dollar, is
bound to succeed.

It is not the employer who pays the
wages. Employees only handle the
money. It is the customer who pays
the wages.

You can't build a reputation on what
you are going to do.

Obstacles are those frightful things
you see when you take your eyes
off your goal.

The object of education, as I see it, is
not to fill a man's mind with facts, it
is to teach him how to use his mind in
thinking. One may fill his head with
all the "facts" of all the ages – and his
head may be just an overloaded fact-
box when he is through.

Before everything else, getting ready is
the secret of success.

Nothing is particularly hard if you
divide it into small jobs.

There are no dead ends. There is
always a way out. What you learn
in one failure you utilize in your
next success.

Only industry and agriculture can
abolish poverty; they can give the
only security human beings can know
– the security of being able and free to
produce what they need. We can do
things in this country because we are
free to do them.

Thinking is the hardest work there is,
which is probably the reason why so
few engage in it.

Only when things are produced in
quantity at the lowest cost and of the best
quality and sold at the narrowest margin
of profit, can we hope for real prosperity.

Progress consists in a number of
related things changing together
for the better.

There is a joy in work. There is
no happiness except in the realization
that we have accomplished something.

A cheaply made product is too
expensive to be priced cheaply.

You will find men who want to be carried
on the shoulders of others, who think
that the world owes them a living. They
don't seem to see that we must all lift
together and pull the weight.

We are accustomed to say, out of
long observation and experience,
that it is not prosperity that makes
the automobile, so much as it is the
automobile that makes prosperity.
It gives a momentum and diversity
to the people's activity which tends
constantly to increase and is most
difficult to stop.

There isn't a person anywhere that
isn't capable of doing more than he
thinks he can.

The genius of the American people is
self-reliance. The old principles that
made us great – self-direction and self-
help – are still contemporary and valid.